Earth our only Home

The purpose of this work is to enlighten the reader with environmental information.

By Mervyn George-Bryan MD

Christian, Business & Health Author
Aloe Naturopath – Medical Masseur,
Lecturer, Member International Aloe Science Council
(Researcher, Nutritional Medicine) (Dip. Health & Nutrition)
(VTCT Holistic Therapies & Swedish Massage.) (Aloe Naturopath.)

http://www.healthlifepublications.com
http://www.healthlifecentre.co.uk

Index

Planet Earth our Only Home

Planet earth contains only so much land. For generations now, the planet has been placed under the pressure caused by two separate and yet integrated changes.

The population growth on the planet

The growth of expectations of the individuals on the planet

Nation states are all trying to increase the wealth of the individual to create the feel good concept of being able to purchase an ever increasing amount of material wealth. Whether this material wealth is the latest television, smart phone, computer, electronic book or the most up to date clothing doesn't matter to the planet. This growth of urbanisation and cultural scientific increase in material wealth and ever increasing complex machines is in fact destroying the very place in which we live; **Planet Earth**.

In the United Kingdom, added to material growth and prosperity, the government of the early 21st century used debt and population growth to fuel economic growth. The fact is that the 60,000,000 people now living in the British Isles would starve if the importation of food and fuel were cut off. Utilising natural growing techniques, which the planet can sustain, would in fact comfortably feed between 30,000,000 and 40,000,000 people. The 40,000,000 figure can only be reached if the whole population became vegetarian. The reason for this is that it takes three times the amount of land to produce 1 kilogram of meat than it does to feed ourselves the equivalent amount of vegetable, grain and fruit based nutrition.

Over the past 400 years Britain has lost over 90% of its forests. World wide the same has taken place. Unfortunately most of the areas that have been deforested to supply our ever increasing appetite for wealth are turning into deserts. This is especially so in areas that were rain forest. 2000 years ago many Northern areas of Africa were agriculturally productive and were covered to a great extent in forest. We can see this as Roman cities and dried out river beds can be found in the middle of the Sahara desert. In fact the deserts of northern Africa are continuing to increase in size. As this increase continues world wide, so more and more agricultural land is lost. Yet the population of the world that depends on this ever decreasing area of productive land is increasing. It has now reached around 7 Billion.

The end result of this equation is clear to be seen, starvation.

The result of the above is simple arithmetic. The planet needs to return to a sustainable agriculture, otherwise there will be a catastrophe such as we cannot comprehend take place on the planet. Alongside of which reforestation must take place to rebalance the eco structure of the planet.

The other major factor that the above has also caused, is an unnatural growth in greenhouse gases which are causing undue climate change and global warming on an unsustainable level.

Not only has industrialization caused an unprecedented amount of carbon gases to be deposited in the atmosphere, but also we see chemical toxins and waste material being deposited in the land and sea. To the extent that vast areas of the oceans are literally being killed by our poisons. Our industrialisation, rather than being productive, is producing a greater amount of waste than useful material.

The ice at the poles which had stored a great deal of the planets water resources is now melting so fast that within 20 years the poles will contain very limited amount of ice. So much so that the sea level rises and consequential flooding predicted will lessen the planets agricultural land. In fact, the annual flooding now taking place around the world is already affecting the inability of once productive agriculture to produce much needed food.

So what is the answer to this terrible dilemma?

On an International and National Scale:-

➤ A reduction in the population of the planet to a sustainable level.

➤ A change of our economic strategies from ever increasing growth to a reduction in material hard ware production by producing products with an extended lifespan, and viewing growth as based on an increase in the welfare of society and use of land, rather than on material and fiscal gain.

➤ A change in the utilisation of resources on the planet so that a more environmentally friendly balance of renewable sources may be utilised.

➤ A reforestation on a scale that will help to replenish the natural eco systems and oxygenate our atmosphere bringing about a more natural balance of the earth.

➤ Using only a three trees planted for each one that is harvested policy worldwide, utilising growing and harvesting methods that are sustainable.

➤ Harvesting trees in small strips so that the natural eco system is not too badly damaged. Thus allowing the natural balance to return quickly.

➤ The use of only natural food growing methods whilst utilising mechanisation that is nature friendly.

➤ The greening of arid and desert lands such as that done by Israel. Firstly concentrating on the southward advance of the Sahara Desert in North and Central Africa.

On a personal Basis Follow the 4 RU's:-

Reducing waste	**Use eco-friendly products**
Re-use	**Use products from sustainable resources**
Recycle	**Use fair traded products**
Reduce energy usage	**Use Low Carbon transport**

Reducing waste where possible by thinking about what we buy and how we use things. Nonessential documents and emails will not be printed. We will endeavour to avoid disposable cups and food packaging. We will ensure all our printing and photocopying is done on double-sided paper. We will ensure that all waste and by-products shall be disposed of in an environmentally friendly manner.

Re-use wherever possible by trying to find a second life for items especially paper and office stationery. Scrap paper will be used in printers, fax machines, for taking messages and for writing notes or draft copies of documents. We are committed to the re-use of envelopes and packaging where possible. When furniture is no longer needed, if it is in good condition, we can advertise it on the free recycle web sites or local schemes available.

Recycling. All waste paper, card, glass, plastic and metal will be recycled. Food waste will be composted. Toner cartridges and inkjets will also be recycled. If office furniture or IT equipment is being replaced then we will seek to have those items reused or recycled. We will use and support social economy organisations to recycle materials as appropriate.

Reduce Energy Usage. This can be by means of utilising energy saving light bulbs and turning lights off when the light from them is not needed for use. Or if a room in the house is not in use, such as a spare bedroom, the heating can be switched off.

Use eco-friendly products. When purchasing products, goods and food we will look on the label to see if it has an environmentally friendly logo applied to it. Organic food for instance is less damaging to the environment than foods grown by chemical fertiliser as well as being healthier for us. We will look for furnishings built of timber from sustainable sources and where possible natural means such as stone and timber in preference to plastics and hybrids. Linen, Wool and Cotton are all natural products that we can use and are healthier for our body than the many synthetics available.

Use products from sustainable resources. Sustainable sources are those which do not reduce the recourses of the planet. Stone is in ample abundance and when finished with remains stone which can be reused. Timber from sustainable forests are now being grown more frequently and is becoming more widely available. A sustainable forest is one where each tree that is chopped down is replanted with one of more trees to replace it.

Use fair traded products. Throughout the world there still remains the use of almost slave labour, with children and adults working in some countries for next to nothing, to provide us with cheap clothing and food. The fair trade logo on our food and clothing label is evidence of an effort to eliminate these inequalities.

Use Low Carbon transport. There are a number of ways that we can lessen our transport environmental impact on the planet. Using public transport where possible, or better yet, walking and cycling. Walking and cycling are also the most healthy modes of transport available. Aircraft travel is the most damaging to the environment. Car transport is next, although in recent years progress has been made in reducing carbon exhaust emissions. Hybrid and electric vehicles are slowly becoming more widely available. The fuel cell electric car being the most eco friendly vehicle now available.

These 4RU's have been developed as a basis to help individuals and groups of all kinds, national institutions, educational institutes and business to become more environmentally friendly and aware.

Environmental Causes and Effects

It is true that there are historical evidences to demonstrate that our planet actually goes through slight changes in world surface temperatures, warming up and cooling on a natural gradual cycle. In the 1700's the river Thames used to freeze over on an annual basis. Further back, 2000 years ago grapes are known to have been grown as far north as York. The Sahara desert on the other hand sustained an agricultural society as is evidenced by the ruins of Roman cities and the dried out river beds. The 21st century difference is that manmade carbon emissions are adding to this process and speeding up the process. The results of which we are beginning to see in excessive weather patterns such as heavy rain over prolonged periods which cause flooding, tornadoes, not just in tornado alley USA but even here in the UK. Hurricanes are becoming more frequent and more powerful.

When I was a child in the 1950's, it was normal for there to be snow frozen on the ground for up to three months each year. It was expected. Now we seldom see snow for more than a few hours at a time. So I can personally testify to the fact that during my life time, temperatures have rises.

The Western World, quickly being followed by the emerging nations, is heavily reliant on power supplied from coal, oil and gas. On top of which, in the UK we have a national power grid which absorbs two thirds more electricity than we actually use in our homes and in industry. The cabling of the national grid actually acts as a giant electric fire heating up the atmosphere. On top of which industry, transport and household pressures each add their own toll.

In areas of traditional forestation, the logging to meet our growing population requirements is causing soil erosion followed by the inevitable prolonged flooding. Then we have heat waves making whole areas of productive agricultural land unproductive. We are finding in England insects which have emigrated here from warmer climates and are now causing problems with our indigenous species.

All of which when combined together is causing an unnatural change in our climate, with unforeseen results.

The evidences for changes caused by this unnatural global warming is resulting in 150000 unnecessary deaths each year and will proliferate in the future, bringing tremendous hardships upon whole communities and even nations.. The extinction of up to a third of land based species is now expected within the next 50 years. In fact, if we continue as we are now, by the year 2100 the planet will be hotter than global records indicate it has ever been before.

 As we utilise the planet's carbon reserves, and cut down its remaining forests, greenhouse gases are pouring into the atmosphere. Hence the delicate balance of atmospheric gases that sustains life is being destroyed, trapping more heat and irreversibly changing our world.

But not all is doom and gloom. The means for reducing the unnatural global warming is known. The decentralisation of energy, cutting our national grid wastage can not only reduce our green house emissions by more than a half, but also reduce our emissions without the need to use the dangerous option nuclear means. Added to which Europe is already producing and has plans to extend its use of water and air power production. The use of our rivers as sources of water power is long overdue. On top of which the change of transports long term reliance on fossil fuels is no longer a problem. Already fossil burning vehicles are changing and becoming less polluting, while alternatives are already available. The lagging of our buildings can add to our efficiency. Utilising existing technology, along with the emergence of greater technological means can make a difference, even at this late hour.

Individuals, business and governments need to be aware of what we can all to together to make a difference. We can all take action to save the planet and at the same time save ourselves money. That's right, a long term reduction in costs can be created by the utilisation of known technologies. Solar panels may cost up front, but can save us a fortune during the life time of this technology. Added to which thermal panels can help heat our water. When building new homes, the inclusion of these technologies along with under floor heating can reduce the foreseeable power consumption in a home, thus saving its residents up to 70% in fuel costs. Our present UK government (2014) has signified its realisation of the problem and its solutions, but is restricted by personal, industrial and national pressures in what it can do. We all need to act together to help solve this problem.

Recognising the problem is the first step in this process. Hence the work being done by the Telford Environmental Centre in providing information and hence an understanding of the situation.

The following Web page by Greenpeace demonstrates how an eco-friendly city can be built.

http://www.greenpeace.org.uk/files/efficiencity/index.html

Energy

Scientists often describe energy as 'the power to bring about change'. However, whichever way you look at it, with regard to energy we need change. Our sources of the carbon based fuels we use to create energy is running out. Hence, our very survival depends on change.

The energy sector accounts for almost half of the UK's carbon emissions. On top of which two thirds of all energy coming out of the UK's power stations is lost as waste heat. Firstly as steam coming out of our cooling towers, and secondly as heat generated by the electricity travelling down our national grid. We can counter this by harvesting this heat by piping the steam from the power stations into the homes as a form of heating and secondly by utilising smaller localised Combined Heat and Power (CHP) plants. A number of countries around the world are already doing this; the UK needs to follow their example and undergo this energy revolution. With a decentralised energy system based on renewable technologies, we could double the efficiency of our power stations, slash our carbon emissions and reduce our reliance on foreign gas. It will then not be necessary to be thinking the unthinkable dangerous idea of going nuclear.

While our governments claim to care about the climate, in fact they have bowed to the demands of corporate business. The government has fallen for the nuclear industry's spin and decided that the UK needs new nuclear power stations. However, nuclear power can't stop climate change or ensure energy security. On top of which until new technology exists regarding the nuclear waste and the way nuclear plants operate, they are a danger to all life. We have two recent examples of nuclear disasters. Chernobyl in 1986 and Fukushima being the best known. These disasters have made agricultural production unfit for human consumption, dependent on wind speed and direction for hundreds of miles. In fact there is a long list of nuclear disasters which have not been made public.

In Japan 12, United Kingdom 3, India 6, Germany 3, France 12, Canada 8, United States of America 45.

More details can be found at the web site

http://en.wikipedia.org/wiki/List_of_nuclear_power_accidents_by_country

There are other national schemes which could be utilised to lessen our need of carbon creating energy production. Hydro power from waves and tides is a major consideration. A series of submerged hydro power units should be in every possible fast flowing river and tidal affected bay and estuary.

We are already seeing a great deal of activity in wind technology. But wind power is not a consistently reliable production method. It depends on wind speeds, too little wind or too much wind and we get no production. However tidal and river power production is consistently reliable. So much for a brief overview of the national and international scene. How about what we as individuals can do.

Personal Use

So much for production, what about usage. There are energy saving light bulbs in plenty now available and in fact this is one area that governments in Europe are acting on. Switching to energy efficient light bulbs will reduce power consumption in the UK by 2%.

Then the electronic equipment that is being produced, such as televisions and computers need to be designed to be switched off completely. Although the stand by mode of such equipment utilises very little power, when the millions of machines left on stand by mode are taken into account, the energy utilised is a vast waste of our natural resources, apart from the excess carbon emissions they cause to be used. If everyone in the Uk were to switch machines off when not in use, we could save a further 4.5% – 5% on our energy consumption. Saving many homes between £60 - £100 a year in fuel costs. In all, with just these two adjustments to our lifestyle, change our light bulbs and switching appliances off when they are not in use, many people can save over £100 a year on fuel bills and the nation can reduce its carbon emissions by 7% or more.

In addition to these small changes to the way we use equipment, and the equipment that we do use, there are other more outstanding changes that can be made. The use of solar panels to produce electricity is well established, while thermal panels can heat our hot water supply to a minimum of 28 degrees centigrade without fuel costs. There are grants available and many companies will actually install this equipment free of charge for you providing you with a reduced fuel bill. Dependent on the initial outlay, the use of this technology can provide you with free electricity. For more information regarding these possibilities, see the web site http://www.energysavingtrust.org.uk

The energy discussion does not end here. In fact it encompasses every aspect of our society. Above we have demonstrated how the UK, and come to that every Western nation could meet the agreed savings in carbon emissions, without the need for nuclear energy production.

There is a fallacy regarding the use of coal. Many organisations see coal as an enemy. However, with the modern filtering equipment, coal can be as clean a technology as gas for the production of energy. Added to which we have an abundance of usable coal in the UK for the foreseeable future. If we use the methods mentioned above, the use of our natural national resources such as coal will not negate our carbon offsetting. To which we already see carbon offsetting being utilised by the use of other renewable fuels such as straw and wood chip materials. The power station at Iron Bridge is one example of what can be done.

Carbon Offsetting

Just a few words about Carbon Offsetting. Greenpeace claim that this idea is simply a way for the industrialised nations to continue using carbon fuels with a clean conscience. Let's see exactly what the UK government says about it. A PDF can be found at:-
http://www.direct.gov.uk/prod_consum_dg/groups/dg_digitalassets/@dg/@en/documents/digitalasset/dg_186202.pdf

It puts it this way

"Calculate – the first action is always to calculate your carbon emissions or the carbon emissions from your organisation. Common emission sources are electricity and gas use and transport. A number of emissions calculators exist – the Government's preferred calculator for individuals is the Act on CO2 Carbon Calculator available at www.direct.gov.uk/ActOnCO2. For organisations, the Carbon Trust has a carbon calculator available at www.carbontrust.co.uk . Both calculators use the latest conversion factors and provide advice on how to reduce your emissions.

Avoid – Once you know the size of your carbon footprint you can begin to take action on CO2. Many emissions can be avoided in the first place for example by finding alternatives to travelling or turning off equipment when it is not in use. Reduce – Once all reasonable actions have been taken to avoid emissions, you should take action to reduce your remaining emissions through efficiency measures, such as using low-energy light bulbs or installing better insulation. Again, both the Act on CO2 Calculator and the Carbon Trust can advise on avoiding and reducing emissions.

Offset – Many emissions cannot currently be avoided or reduced. You could consider offsetting some or all of these remaining emissions. Offset providers will help you to calculate the emissions relating to the particular activities you wish to offset. If you're not sure where to buy your offsets, the Quality Assurance Scheme for carbon offsetting will make it easy for you to identify good quality offsets. If you don't purchase quality assured offsets, then you should take the time to check that the offsets you choose represent real CO2 reductions and have been measured and verified by a competent third party."

Simply put, you can continue to produce a carbon footprint as long as you can find someone who is utilising a lesser carbon footprint to balance your use. I agree with Greenpeace, in one way it's a con. On the other hand it may produce some good as it makes organisations think about their carbon footprint, which may in turn focus people's minds on the need to reduce their carbon footprint and in turn focus people's minds on ways to actually achieve this.

Greening Business

Or what Business and Industry can do to help.

Renewable technologies such as wind turbines, solar panels and heat exchange units are effective alternatives to fossil fuels and will help you to meet our energy requirements and also reduce our carbon dioxide emissions. Renewables can help us to replace our dependence on fossil fuel based energy sources which contribute to global warming, and are susceptible to price fluctuations and have a finite life span.

For instance, the super store firms such as Tesco, Morrison's, Sainsbury's and Asda to name but a few, have roof space above their stores to install solar panels thus offsetting the electricity they use in lighting, refrigerators and freezers. In fact with that type of roof space available to them, they could potentially become producers on the open market, adding production to the electricity grid and earning. If all the firms that have that type of roof space were to utilise it in this way, the need for new expensive or even nuclear electricity supply would be lessened in one stroke.

Friends of the Earth have a Business Partnership program that enables some of the following areas of help in environmental management. They take into account, Development and implementation of ISO14001, BS8555, BS EN16001 and ISO9001:2008.

Their aim is to work in harmony with business to reduce production costs while lessening the carbon footprint of companies. There is also support available from the UK

Environmental Agency

https://www.gov.uk/government/topics/environment

Energy Saving Trust.

http://www.energysavingtrust.org.uk/

There is management and staff training available to organisations. The more people's minds are focussed on the problem, the more solutions will be found and more will be done. Other web sites of interest are:-

Carbon Trust

http://www.carbontrust.co.uk/Pages/Default.aspx

Provide help for business

Global Action Plan

http://www.globalactionplan.org.uk/

A Charity which offers help to business, especially around the office is**Greening the Office**

http://www.green-office.org.uk/

Organisations also have a significant role to play in forest protection and management. By using only timber and paper that comes from environmentally responsible and socially just forest management, they can have a huge impact on the rate of deforestation.

This isn't just limited to businesses dealing directly in timber products. With agriculture being a major cause of deforestation, food manufacturers and retailers also need to make sure their products are not being grown in newly deforested areas.

Health

Natural catastrophes initiated or enhanced by global warming such as Heat waves, severe storms, air pollution, and diseases linked to climate already threaten people's health in many areas of the world. The increase in these will engulf all nations on the globe. The excuse utilized by developing nations that they want what the Western World already have is understandable, but all nations must make sacrifices if a global catastrophe is to be averted. In fact the underdeveloped nations will be affected in a greater way than the developed. As the developed world has the infrastructure to help it cope with some of the results. Not only will natural events become more destructive, but people's health will be affected. Those in greatest risk will be the poor, infants, the young the elderly and the disabled. Those who live in coastal areas or big cities will become more affected as time progresses.

Already heat waves are affecting whole areas of the planet causing droughts, starvation, or simply uncomfortable for everyone. Illnesses such as heat cramps, heat stroke, and even death are becoming more common. A 2003 heat wave in Europe caused about 50,000 deaths, and a 1995 heat wave in Chicago caused more than 600 deaths. In fact, heat waves cause more deaths in the United States every year than hurricanes, tornadoes, floods, and earthquakes combined.

Air pollution is causing more and more problems. I have personally suffered with Asthma since childhood. When I was a young boy, no one else in school had asthma. Now however one in three children in the UK are said to have asthma. Why this increase? Especially taking into account the fact that the clean air acts of 1956 and 1968 have apparently cleaned up our environment. Unfortunately the fumes from diesel vehicles contain a molecule that aggravates the bronchia initiating asthma.

Another modern pollutant that aggravates asthma is the lower ozone created by invisible chemical reactions in our lower atmosphere. Ozone found high in the atmosphere protects the planet from harmful rays emitted from the sun. As the use of chemicals and manufacturing of plastics proliferates, so does this harmful lower ozone.

Already in the UK birds, animals and especially insects, some of which are dangerous to our health, are finding their way into our eco system. Mosquitoes and ticks attack human beings, while larger insect have been recently found in the UK that attack our cattle and even the humble honey bee.

Agriculture

The crops that we grow for food need specific conditions to thrive, including the right temperature, enough light and water. One of the causes for the increase in global warming is the manufacture of chemical based fertilisers. The use of natural occurring fertilisers and soil bulking and balancing humus and organic matter will increase the ability of the soil to absorb the effects of climate change and to enable it to continue to produce food crops. Humus and organic matter in the soil is driven out by the use of highly acidic chemical fertilisers. Which in turn lessens the ability of the soil to retain water, and hence increase the likelihood of flooding.

Climate could have both positive and negative effects on crops.

Warmer weather in northern climate can enable the growth of crops not before grown in certain areas, while at the same time warmer southern areas will be adversely affected with the creation of yet more desert like conditions as water levels will in some areas drop, while in other areas water proliferation will cause flooding. As we saw in 2014 on the Somerset plains in England, whole areas of once agriculturally rich land was laid waste by flooding, affecting the crops that had been sowed. In fact, as I write this in June 2014 the water table is so high the rain fall is causing flooding. According to government statistics we can expect a decrease in crop production, especially grain production of between 10% and 30% in the next ten years. In the lower Himalayas we have seen how the deforestation is affecting not just the agriculture of that region, with the loss of local crop growing, but the flooding and total devastation of crop growing in the lower regions, especially in Bangladesh; as the areas are now regularly flooded, completely wiping out the ability of that area to be agriculturally productive. Similar problems are occurring in many parts of the world. Especially in the Amazon basin. Another area being affected by business demands is Indonesia where palm oil growing is on the increase. Rain forests are being depleted to make room for the crops of palm oil, which is not only affecting the forest, but also the multitude of animals including tigers, elephants and orangutans. Within years of the rain forests being depleted, the land becomes infertile and a desert. So it is that while the human population is booming, the productive land for food is diminishing. The end result is obvious to any thinking person. We are already seeing it in parts of Africa where droughts are causing malnutrition. Another problem is that the food reserves in the West that were once plentiful have now diminished and hence the crops that were once sent to areas where starvation was taking place, no longer exist.

Animals and plants live in climates that are conducive to their existence. As the climate is warming up, they tend to migrate north and also to cooler areas higher up. This in turn puts pressure on the native species of these more northern or higher areas. In fact whole ecosystems are being affected, which in turn affects neighboring areas and hence the problem accumulates. Another problem is the natural life cycle of life. As the climate warms up, so the growth patterns change with plants growing earlier in the season, with a problem when frost does appear, as it naturally does in those earlier months. Plants are damaged and killed, with farmers having to reseed areas where possible increasing costs and lessening the harvest.

So what can be done about it:-

Soil Maintenance

Farmers can utilize natural bulking agents and fertilisers that will replenish the soil, not just make plants grow and look good. In this way the soil on which our survival hinges will be able to accommodate change and the high winds which are otherwise blowing off the dust from areas such as east Anglia. Instead of burning off the stubble, farmers have already started to plough it back into the soil as a bulking agent. This needs to be done elsewhere so that the soil is able to regenerate. Around the corner from where I am right now, in Telford, England, there are fields that have been used to grow rape seed, year in, year out for the past 20 years. The farmers rely in chemical fertilisers to feed the plants with. Not only does this diminish the nutritional base of the crop, but the soil has lost its consistence, becoming year on year more like sand. The lighter grains of soil being blown away by the wind and washed away by the rain. Unless bulking agents are utilized, the ability of the soil to sustain growth will diminish.

Farming

There are crops such as barley and oats which are very nutritious that can be utilized for human consumption, rather than animal feed. It takes three times as much grain to produce one unit of animal protein as it does to produce plant based protein for human consumption. There are now plant based protein foods which are actually richer in nutrients than animal based proteins, cost less to produce and are friendlier to the environment than the production of animal based foods. Pre sprouited barley flour is 40 times higher in active nutrients than best prime steak. I have heard farmers argue that their land is only suitable for animal production, especially the hills. However, although grain crops utilizing mechanization may not be possible, the growth of other quick growing annual crops which can be harvested as fuel may be possible. Also, crops needing less mechanization can also be grown. Then we also have reforestation. If the hills can grow grass, they can grow many other crops, including of course, trees. I realize that whole communities and ways of life will be affected by these changes, but which is better, the total loss of our living environment and worldwide starvation and ill health, or learning new skills?

As the climate changes, there are plants which previously would not grow in northern areas, which now can, and with careful management can be introduced into the eco system.

Gardening

Gardens are becoming more important as areas of the surrounding ecosystems. They can with the right management become an area in which biodiversity for insects, birds and animals to live in. The flowers and vegetables can attract insects, including the bee, upon which food production as a whole is so reliant.

Natural composting of waist food and plant materials can lessen the impact of humanity upon the planet by reducing wastage and replenishing the soil naturally. Working the land is also a healthy pastime, relaxing and at the same time physically enhancing.

The Organic and Locality discussion.

Is it better for our health and for the sake of the environment to eat organic food where possible and locally grown produce. The answer is clearly, yes.

Firstly organic use of the land is beneficial to it and the food is less likely to contain the harmful chemicals that are sprayed onto our normal crops. Next the food is proven to be more beneficial nutritionally than that grown by high intensive farming. Vegetation of all types can only contain the nutrients that it is able to gain from the soil in which it is grown. In Britain, there has been a natural need to increase our crop yield as the population has increased. After the second world war in 1945 the government decided to help develop ways in which crop yield could be increased, so that the population could be fed. This has through its evolutionary processes developed into the highly mechanized intensive farming of today.

Next, locally grown food simply does not have to be transported as far as other crops. Hence there is less transport pollution and transport costs are less. The normal crop distribution includes the following. Transport from the farm to a packaging centre. Next that packaging process itself takes time. Then transport to the supermarket distribution takes place, after which transport to the supermarkets is needed. All in all crops distributed in this way can be transported hundreds of miles, whereas if the food is grown and purchased locally, costs and transport pollution can be kept to a minimum. Also, the more time vegetables and fruit take from the point of harvest to the table, the less nutritional value they contain. Within 48 hours of harvest, most fruit and vegetables can lose up to 70% of their nutritional value. The loss is caused by oxidization the natural process of oxygen acting upon the plant. We can lessen this by freezing and vacuum packing. However these are costly, but in a compromise situation freezing is probably the lesser of evils. The best option is to purchase locally grown foods. Many green grocer shops are making contact with local farmers and purchasing directly from them. Though the crops may not be so nicely displayed as the factory packaged crops, they are better for us and the little time and effort it takes us to prepare them is beneficial to us, both nutritionally and environmentally.

Forests

Most of our planet was until relatively recent times covered in ancient forests. The forests were our natural home. About two thirds of all animal and plant species are found in the forests. Millions of people still depend on these forests for their existence. They are also a vital aspect of the planets eco system. Along side the oceans they help regulate our climate. Without them desertification and death will follow.

In the past 2000 years over 80% of our ancient forests have been destroyed, and half of that in the last 30 years. The planet cannot continue to sustain life as we know it, if this rate of destruction is continued. Illegal and destructive logging, industrial-scale farming and, increasingly, climate change (partly caused by deforestation in the first place) all threaten the remaining forests. thousands of species of animals and plants face extinction.

Timber is in greater demand now than it ever has been. As the planets human population continues to explode, the pressure on our forests becomes intolerable. Timber for building, furniture, books, toilet rolls and so on is ever increasing. Farming is also an ever increasing reason for deforestation. As the pressure for more and more food is placed on the market, ever increasing areas of virgin forest is being depleted and burned to make way for agriculture. The need for soya and palm oil are two of the most often grown crops on these areas.In some areas such as the Amazon, slave labour is still in use.

Sixty million indigenous people depend on forests for their survival, while a further 1.6 billion make their livelihoods from forest products.

Destructive and illegal logging

There have been a few attempts by governments to control logging; however the lack of policing has allowed increasing illegal activities.

Climate change

Forests store carbon and control water recycling on the planet. The deforestation is releasing nearly 20% of all carbon into the atmosphere, more than that of all the global transport. If this deforestation continues at its present rate, the inevitable consequences will overwhelm us.

Protected Forests   Less than 8% of the planets rain forests are protected. So we can see that huge areas of rain forest are under threat. This is despite the fact that nation states in which these forests exist know that the forests depletion will eventually destroy their habitat. Unfortunately politicians take a short term view on the subject. There needs to be serious work done in protecting all of the forest that is left, and a reintroduction of forest on the land from which it has been depleted. It has been demonstrated that within a relatively few years with careful management, rain forest can be re-introduced, starting on the edges of the existing forest working outward. If a cut one tree down, plant 3 trees policy were adopted worldwide, as we see in taking place in Northern Europe, the problem of deforestation could be solved, and the nation states in which this forest exists could continue earn much needed revenue for its populace. When new hard wood is required from virgin forest, (it taking hundreds of years to grow) strip farming and replanting as the harvesting is done, is the answer. This form of logging helps to maintains a rain forest eco system and at the same time give the local population work.

Bio Diversity

Once the rain forest trees are reintroduced on the edge of existing forest, or in strip harvesting, the bio diversity very quickly grows back. The lower bush and animals very quickly come back. In this way we can retain the multitude of plant and animal life. This is important as the environment of the whole planet is affected each time we lose a species.

Areas of experiment in reintroducing rain forest in this way, which have already taken place; have demonstrated that within 20 years the natural biodiversity can be restored.

Government action   Government action by the involved nation states is required, with the Western nations which have the technology and expertise need to give them their full support. Both financially and in training. In the meantime Western nation states can introduce legislation banning the importation of illegally or none environmentally friendly harvested timber. This would make those involved establish an eco-friendly friendly system. Something that is necessary to slow down global warming, which along with other measures in manufacturing and transport can help lessen the release of carbon and the resultant increase in global warming.

Changing industry practices

All business can have a significant influence in reducing the rate of deforestation by only purchasing timber and paper products that comes from environmentally responsible forest. Look for the Forest Stewardship Council FSC logo on the product that you are purchasing. Food manufacturers also need to check whether or not the products they are purchasing come from areas that are deforested or not. Once the message gets out onto the market place, the source suppliers will stop deforesting as it will not pay them to do so.

Areas of forest in the world are unfortunately it is being destroyed at the rate of the size of Wales each year. Not only for logging purposes, but also to clear the land for agricultural purposes. Corruption is endemic with illegal clearance taking place. All firms involved in the production of food, whether for human or animal feed, need to send out the message loud and clear. WE DO NOT PURCHASE PRODUCTS GROWN AT THE EXPENCE OF THE FOREST. After all, the wellbeing of humanity and the animal kingdom depends on the oxygenation and biodiversity that these forests provide. Other large areas of forest in the world are:-

- The Amazon rainforest
- The Congo rainforest of central Africa
- The Paradise Forests of South East Asia
- The Boreal Forest of Canada
- Europe and Russia

We all, each of us have a role to play in the protection of the rain forest. The construction industry is the biggest consumer of timber in the country. Whether it be in building, furnishing or in the garden. The use of FSC certified products will help to maintain the eco systems that are so vital to our wellbeing. Books, magazines and toilet tissue also play their part.

Recycled paper

Using recycled paper production reduces the amount of waste going to landfill, reduces the amount of timber being harvested, uses less energy than paper made directly from timber sources.

In the home we can:

- **Use e-mail when possible**
- **Print on both sides of the paper**
- **Use local recycling facilities**

Remember the 4 RU's

Reducing waste	Use eco friendly products
Re-use	Use products from sustainable resources
Recycle	Use fair traded products
Reduce energy usage	Use Low Carbon transport

Fair Trade

Always look for the Fairtrade logo as this ensures that decent wages and fair work conditions are paid to the workers and because harmful pesticides are forbidden, the end product is likely to be environmentally friendly. Imported fruit and drinks such as tea, coffee and chocolate are the main food items to look for.

We can also help by looking for the fairtrade logo on furnishings and decorating materials that are imported.

The Oceans

Life on this planet is totally dependent on water. We could manage it a bit more wisely. Do you know, for example, that the average Spaniard uses 250 litres of water a day, while a tourist in Spain uses on average 880 litres? Our waste products also so often end up being dumped into the ocean. Although great improvements have already been made in cleaning up sewerage before it goes into the sea, there is ample room for more improvements. Some industries are still discharging toxic waste into our water systems.

Apart from the quality of water, global climate change threatens coastlines and the buildings and cities located along them. Hundreds of millions of people around the world live in low–lying areas near the coast that could be flooded as the sea level rises. Rising sea level is already eroding beaches and damaging many coastal areas.. Rising sea level and stronger storms caused by warmer oceans could completely wipe out certain beaches and islands. Already in the United Kingdom erosion is costing people their homes as cliffs collapse and houses fall into the sea. It has been estimated that whole areas of coastline could be overwhelmed.

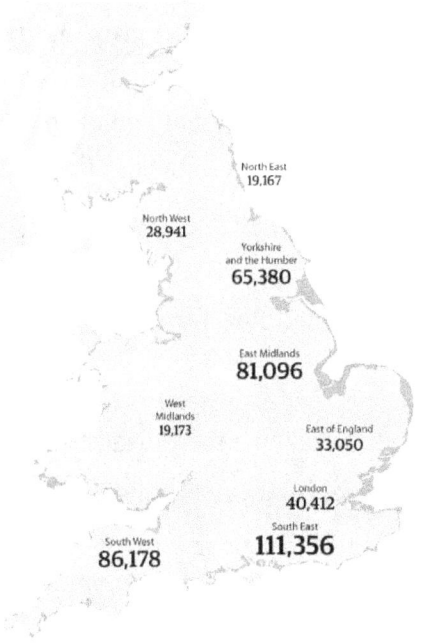

This picture illustrates the areas at risk in the Uk by 2050 if the present rate of glacial melt continues, with the resultant ocean rises. Other areas of the world along the east coast of the USA and mainland Europe along with low lying islands are in far greater danger.

Another area of interest affecting our oceans is that of fishing. Over fishing and wasteful fishing practices are laying whole areas of the ocean unproductive. The natural food chain of Whale down to plankton is being disrupted. This is of vital importance because, alongside our forests, the oceans provide our oxygen.

Climate change with the resultant warming of the oceans is already affecting coral, with whole reefs dying as their environmental systems upon which their life depends is being destroyed. If this continues at its present rate, whole areas of productive ocean will have died, with unknown effects on the planets eco systems.

Transport

Transport is responsible for 22 per cent of the UK's carbon emissions, and vehicles in the UK are pumping out more greenhouse gases than ever before. At the moment, EU car manufacturers only have a voluntary agreement to reduce the emissions of their cars. To make real progress towards low carbon cars, binding efficiency targets need to be imposed on manufacturers and gas-guzzlers need to be discouraged.

Aviation is the fastest growing cause of climate change in the world, and the popularity of short haul flights is still growing. According to the Tyndall Centre, if air traffic is allowed to keep growing at its present rate, then all other sectors will have to reduce their emissions to zero in order to reach the government's climate change targets. The EU and governments urgently needs to make flying less friendly.

The Petrol Diesel Debate

Both fuels have their disadvantages.

The greenest way to travel is by bike, foot or public transport.

Only use your car when it's **absolutely essential** and consider buying a hybrid a pure electric vehicle. Electric vehicles are becoming more popular and are even being raced. Although the electricity to drive the electric car has to come from somewhere, the use of solar, wind and water to generate electricity is helping to cut down the carbon efficiency in electricity production. So far the electric car is by far the best option. The latest electric cars will travel between 200 and three hundred miles, (dependant on terrain and speed) and even on a long haul journey, the motorway and city car parks now have started installing charging points.

Petrol and diesel engines are inefficient. Petrol engines emit more carbon dioxide, carbon monoxide and hydrocarbons.

Diesel engines produce more nitrogen oxides, sulphur dioxide, black smoke and particles - associated with poor urban air quality. These particles along with low lying ozone's are the reason for the increase in asthma and other lung diseases.

Petrol and diesel can be reformulated to cut emissions, e.g. City Diesel / Petrol. The catalytic converter now installed on all motors can also cut emissions from both.

In the past few years the motor manufacturers have made great strides in increasing the efficiency of engines, with a more than halving of fuel use and there for with improvements in engine manufacturing and efficiency, a more than halving of their carbon emissions. In fact on some vehicles the emissions are so low that the UK government tax duty is zero rated. Hence encouraging the driver to purchase such a vehicle.

Transport Costs

The opinion has been put forward that because waste paper is delivered to paper banks, transported for processing and distribution, the energy used will outweigh the benefits of energy savings from the recycling process. This does not take into account the fact that by recycling paper, we are cutting down less trees and therefor carbon absorption by trees is maintained at a higher level than would be if only trees were utilised in the manufacture of paper. Also the energy costs between different transport scenarios of virgin paper and recycled paper are insignificant in comparison to the energy savings arising from the recycled paper production process. The best thing we can do is not to use paper at all. We can save our work as computer files and send letters and files can be sent world wide by email.

The Transport of Food

The Validity of Food Miles as an Indicator of Sustainable Development

Quoting the Final Report produced for DEFRA 2002

Over the last fifty years, there have been dramatic changes in the food production and supply chain in the UK. The most striking changes have been:

♦ Globalisation of the food industry, with an increase in food trade (imports and exports) and wider sourcing of food within the UK and overseas;

♦ Concentration of the food supply base into fewer, larger suppliers, partly to meet demand for bulk year-round supply of uniform produce;

♦ Major changes in delivery patterns with most goods now routed through supermarket regional distribution centres, and a trend towards use of larger Heavy Goods Vehicles (HGVs);

♦ Centralisation and concentration of sales in supermarkets, with a switch from frequent food shopping (on foot) at small local shops to weekly shopping by car at large out of town supermarkets.

These trends have led to a large increase in the distance food travels from the farm to consumer, known as "food miles". Indeed, since 1978, the annual amount of food moved in the UK by HGVs has increased by 23%, and the average distance for each trip has increased by over 50%.
The rise in food miles has led to increases in the environmental, social and economic burdens associated with transport. These include carbon dioxide emissions, air pollution, congestion, accidents and noise. There is a clear cause and effect relationship for food miles for these burdens

– and in general higher levels of vehicle activity lead to larger impacts. Growing concern over these impacts has led to a debate on whether to try to measure and reduce food miles.

The direct environmental, social and economic costs of food transport are over £9 billion each year, and are dominated by congestion. Using standard government methodology, the social cost of congestion, associated with food transport is estimated at £5 billion. This is over 50% of the social costs associated with food transport, and arises from the use of HGVs, LGVs, and cars are associated with food transport in the UK. Accidents lead to social costs of £2 billion per year. Greenhouse gas emissions, air pollution, noise, and
infrastructure cost a further £2 billion. The total costs are very significant compared with the gross value added of the agriculture sector (£6.4 billion), and the food and drink manufacturing sector (£19.8 billion) in 2002. It should be noted that these cost estimates depend on the assumptions and methodology used. For example, the congestion costs are marginal costs, as the impact of an extra kilometre travelled depends on the existing level of traffic. The use of average costs, although not recommended, would give lower values. Also, the costs reflect only immediate impacts. For congestion, these impacts are short term and reversible, whereas climate change impacts are long term and irreversible. It should be stressed that not all impacts are included in this assessment (for example noise, infrastructure and congestion costs from air transport are not quantified).

Food transport has significant and growing impacts. Food transport accounted for an estimated 30 billion vehicle kilometres in 2002, of which 82% are in the UK. Road transport accounts for most of the vehicle kilometres, split between cars, HGVs and LGVs.

Food transport produced **19 million tonnes of carbon dioxide** in 2002, of which 10 million tonnes were emitted in the UK (almost all from road transport), representing 1.8% of the total annual UK CO_2 emissions, and 8.7% of the total emissions of the UK road sector.

Transport of food by air has the highest CO_2 emissions per tonne, and is the fastest growing mode. Although air freight of food accounts for only 1% of food tonne kilometres and 0.1% of vehicle kilometres, it produces 11% of the food transport CO_2 equivalent emissions.

From this research and others now available, it is clear that the modern way of shopping in out of town or even in town retail parks, although enjoyed by individuals, is causing a major impact on carbon and other social factors. The fact that to get to these retail parks we use our cars, very few retail parks being served by public transport, when combined with the long distances that food travels from farm to consumer, which the modern centralised food industry has imposed upon us; food purchasing has become a major factor in climate and negative social change. There is little that the individual can do. However, most areas of the country have small greengrocers that aim to local farmers products. Attending local farmers markets to purchase our food from can also help. The old adage, "Every Little Helps" is still true.

The School Run

Parents using the car to take children to school are a major problem increasing the global warming emissions of transport, causing the social disruption of parking in front of people's properties and the school gates. Many accidents are caused by the school run problem with children crossing roads from between parked vehicles.

Measurements of an increase in atmospheric pollution outside schools caused by the school run can cause detrimental health effects for many children as they leave school, depending on the atmospheric conditions at the time.

According to one survey overall journeys to school made by car are responsible for releasing over 363,075 tons of CO_2 into the atmosphere each year.

Currently over 1,760,000 children are driven to primary school across the UK - even though pupils live an average of 1.8 miles from their school which takes just 20 minutes to bike or scoot.

Many schools have schemes which are helping to decrease the need for the use of motorised transport to and from school. These include the provision of secured bicycle shelters, and the encouraging of parents to support their children in walking, scooting and cycling. Activities usually enjoyed by children.

Solar Roadways"

The idea of this unique invention is the use of panels with inbuilt solar receptors and LED reflectors. The panels are clipped into each other and transmit the electricity that they generate down a duct at the side of the road to the local electricity grid. In return each panel is in receipt of a signal from a central control which enable the LED lights to be switched on to create any sign that is required.

The amount of electricity that a system of roads built in this way can generate is the equivalent to reducing greenhouse gas production by 75%. The inventor an electrical engineer called Scott Brusaw has been developing this idea since 2012 and experiments are ongoing.

These Solar Road Panels which can withstand the heaviest trucks can be installed on roads, parking lots, driveways, sidewalks, bike paths, playgrounds... literally any surface under the sun. They pay for themselves primarily through the generation of electricity, which can power homes and businesses connected via driveways and parking lots. A nationwide system could produce more clean renewable energy than a country uses as a whole. They even send a fault signal to the central control if they become faulty. They are easy to replace the faulty panel being unlocked, lifted and the replacement being locked back into place. Hence the expensive road repair work that costs government billions each year will be done away with and the road builder will instead earn from the electricity generated.

In the United States of America where these experiments are taking place, if the main highways were built in this way, taking into account just 4 hours of good daylight each day, 14.95 Billion Kilowatts of power each year would be generated. This meets up to 75% of the total usage of the country. All in all this idea is a win win situation.

The Levitating Monorail
Designed To Replace Cars

SkyTran is a Personal Rapid Transit (PRT) system originally conceived by aerospace engineer Douglas Malewecki. The idea is to lessen congestion and pollution by providing a rapid transit system for people transit. Sky Tran are working in conjunction with NASA in the production of this system.

It runs silently and is computer controlled to take the passengers from their position to destination without any input from the passengers.

As can be seen by the computerized graphics, it would run on an elevated monorail system and would be a cheaper system than the expensive tramways and high speed rail links being built across nations.

In urban districts, this system would reduce traffic congestion and reduce travel time. When ordering the pod the passengers would fill in their pick up point and time of pick up, number of passengers and destination. The correct sized pod would arrive and take the passengers by the quickest route to their destination. Such a system utilise nationwide would reduce carbon emissions from transport by over 60%.

Our Homes

While it is crucial to start cutting the wastage at our power stations, that doesn't take the onus off the rest of us. Domestic usage accounts for 15 per cent of the UK's carbon emissions. A proportion of this can be cut out by very simple changes to our lives, like switching our light bulbs to energy efficient bulbs, turning off all appliances when we aren't using them and fitting insulation in the loft, floors and walls.

But we can go further. Decentralising our energy system enables homes to become power stations. By installing small scale solar or wind generators we can generate our own power; we could even sell our excess power to our neighbours through the national grid.

There are today various schemes enabling even the less well-off to let their roof space to companies who will install solar panels for free, enabling the householder to have electricity for free or at a reduced cost, while the company earns from the excess electricity produced. In fact, with these schemes available, the roof space on our homes can help everyone to save money and at the same time help reduce the nations carbon emission's.

It is estimated that the initial outlay of installing solar panels can be retrieved after less than 7 years. Most solar panels have a listed life span of over 20 years. From a business and household long term budget, whether you utilise one of the free roof rental schemes or purchase yourself, it makes sense to use your roof space in this way.

Business

Supermarkets, warehouses, offices and factories have enormous roof space to utilise. Not only would the utilisation of roof space lower the companies running costs, but would also in most cases earn the company involved extra income. It's a win win situation.

It has been argued that solar production is not the answer to our electricity needs as it only produces electricity during day light. This is true, but the more solar panels in the grid, the less electricity carbon driven power stations need to produce during day light, thus saving emissions during this time. Day light in mid winter is 8 hours and in mid summer is 16 hours, therefor over the year is averages about 50% of the time.

So why aren't more people jumping on the Solar Panel Band Wagon?

We believe it is simply a lack of knowledge regarding the possibilities. Many people fear that solar panels are too expensive for them. To this end the roof leasing schemes come into play for those who own their own homes. For private and social housing Land Lords, the introduction of solar panels can earn them money as they will become the providers of electricity to their tenants, and also earn them money from the grid from the excess. Over half the properties in the UK have roof space which could be utilised in this way.

Our Lifestyles

Every one of us can green up our lifestyle and for very little effort save ourselves money. The following is a simple list of effective things we can do right now:-

- Make sure we are using energy saving light bulbs
- Turn off equipment when not in use
- Use environmentally friendly materials, natural in preference to chemical based
- Insulate our homes
- Update out of date heating equipment as new boilers will save you money on running costs

Follow our 4 RU's

See page 4 of this report for further information.

Reducing waste	**Use eco-friendly products**
Re-use	**Use products from sustainable resources**
Recycle	**Use fair traded products**
Reduce energy usage	**Use Low Carbon transport**

Gardening

Many of us enjoy gardening and flowers fill our borders with beauty. This is important in helping to balance the natural habitat for insects upon which we rely for pollination, and without which there would be no food production. However there is ample space left in our gardens, no matter how large or small, to grow herbs and many vegetables and fruits.

Replace trees with fruit bearing varieties. For instance, hide your fencing with a border containing runner beans of various varieties, which can produce an abundance of beautiful flowers throughout the summer, and provide healthy meals. Potatoes can be placed at the back of borders, behind your flowers. While every day salad items such as tomatoes, lettuce and cucumbers can be grown in a variety of ways, from window ledge boxes to greenhouses. Many varieties will grow out of doors. Even if you only have a patio, you can utilise grow bags to grow your food in. Many people get a sense of satisfaction from growing their own produce, and it can be fun. Children love to see the seedlings first pop up their heads from the soil. They can also learn to care for the plants, watering them and recognising the difference between plants and weeds. Most schools in the UK now have a garden area and children learn from this the delights of gardening. For the more robust of us, an allotment can be a source of relaxation and food provider.

Don't waste your food. If you have some left over from your meals, put it into the compost bin provided by your council.

Science

Science has taken a cautious approach as many scientists involved have taken some convincing and before they were ready to back the arguments with their understanding and reputations, are only now willing to agree with the evidence which is now overwhelming.

There is a change in our climate which humanity has in its known existence, never before witnessed.

There is ample evidence of changing climates in history, however what we see happening now is much quicker and more violent than ever before in recorded history. Science now agrees that the use of carbon fuels, in transport and providing power for homes and industry is adding to the natural cycles. Hence the extremes in weather we are now seeing.

Politics

The politics (UK)

Until the last few years, politicians, just like scientists were slow to respond to the problem of global warming and environmental change. The present government has started to respond to the needs, but much more needs to be done.

The response to fracking is an example. The arguments for and against are complex, and the need for home produced gas is inescapable. However, as we've already pointed out, with the solar technology, and a greater use of tidal and river power, a great deal of the energy needs of the nation can be reduced. The use of solar on the roof and electric radiators such as those used in Germany, can go a long way to reducing our need to import gas.

The political need for change is unanswerable, yet the power lobbies of the oil and energy giants is restricting the political will.

Greenpeace and Friends of the Earth claim the following:-

The politics (international)

Carbon emissions don't respect borders and the sad fact is that the world's most vulnerable people are the ones that are suffering most from its impacts. With countries like China and India in the middle of their own industrial revolutions, it's clear we need a global framework and global cooperation to address the problem. The Kyoto Protocol is a crucial first step but far, far more needs to be done.

The nuclear distraction

While the government claims to care about the climate, in practice it has bowed to the demands of big business. The government has fallen for the nuclear industry's spin and decided that the UK needs new nuclear power stations. Nuclear power can't stop climate change or ensure energy security. We need to start reducing emissions within a decade to avoid catastrophic climate change; the first new nuclear power stations won't produce a watt of energy before 2018.

Terrorism

Aside from the risk of a terrorist strike directly onto a nuclear power station, the nuclear industry transports thousands of tonnes of radioactive waste around the UK by road, rail and sea. Every week, communities up and down the country are put at risk from potential radioactive contamination as these trains trundle through our cities, towns and villages. There are no police or security personnel on board and there are no local plans in place to deal with an emergency. If a nuclear waste train was involved in a terrorist attack, tens of thousands of people could be exposed to cancer causing radiation and whole regions might have to be evacuated.

The good news is that we know exactly what needs to be done to stop climate change - and the technologies we need already exist. With the right policies at international, national and local levels, we would be able to deploy them on a large scale.

Clean energy

Two thirds of all energy going into the UK's power stations is lost as waste heat - up the chimney and in the cooling towers. If we captured this waste heat, there would be enough of it to heat every building and business in the UK.

To capture and use this heat, we would need to stop relying on our archaic, centralised energy system and start producing energy in smaller, local **combined heat and power (CHP)** plants. A number of countries around the world are already doing this; the UK needs to follow their example and undergo an energy revolution. With a decentralised energy system based on **renewable technologies**, we could double the efficiency of our power stations, slash our carbon emissions and reduce our reliance on foreign gas.

The role of governments and companies

If these threats are so apparent, why have governments not done more to combat them? Simply put, there is a distinct lack of political will on all sides to take action. In the developing world, a lack of funding for management and policing protected areas is aggravated by widespread corruption, while in industrialised nations products made from illegally logged timber are cheaper than those produced in an environmentally and socially responsible way.

Even our own government can't abide by its own guidelines for buying timber- despite verbal commitments towards forest protection, it's still absurdly easy to find products made from illegal and unsustainably logged timber on sale in this country.

United Nations

The United Nations (UN) is an international organization whose stated aims are to facilitate cooperation in international law, international security, economic development, social progress

and human rights issues.
http://www.un.org

We need to reduce greenhouse gas emissions in line with what the science requires. All countries must play a part, based on common but differentiated responsibilities

Secretary-General Ban Ki-moon,
17 August 2009

Ecological Organisations

CARBON TRUST www.carbontrust.co.uk	SSEG www.sseg.org.uk
LowC^{VP} low carbon vehicle partnership — Accelerating the Shift to Low Carbon Vehicles and Fuels www.lowcvp.org.uk	sustainable communities initiatives www.sci-scotland.org.uk
energy saving trust www.energysavingtrust.org.uk	SAVE THE RAIN www.savetherain.info
forum for the future action for a sustainable world www.forumforthefuture.org	globalgiving.co.uk www.globalgiving.co.uk
Friends of the Earth www.foe.co.uk	FSC www.fsc-uk.org stuff for schools
www.green-alliance.org.uk	www.recycle.co.uk recycle stuff on internet www.uk.freecycle.org
Centre for Sustainable Energy www.cse.org.uk	www.activityvillage.co.uk recycle activities for kids
SCOTTISH renewables www.scottishrenewables.com	http://www.google.co.uk/#q=recycle+kids&hl=en&sa=X&prmd=ivns&source=univ&tbs=vid:1&tbo=u&ei=IJoaTbOLIZSxhQfVvti3Dg&oi=video_result_group&ct=title&resnum=8&ved=0CHkQqwQwBw&fp=9d7ce4890fa552ce videos for kids etc recycle etc

Cowrie www.offshorewindfarms.co.uk	Centre for Alternative Technology Canolfan y Dechnoleg Amgen www.cat.org.uk
LOW CARBON NETWORK www.lowcarbon.co.uk Stuff for schools & education	www.ecoliteracy.org school stuff
www.kidsforsavingearth.org usa education nice art work	nicodemus wilderness project www.wildernessproject.org Stuff 4 kids
CONSERVATION INTERNATIONAL www.conservation.org	Global Greenhouse Warming.com http://www.global-greenhouse-warming.com/facts-impacts-climate-change.html
http://www.environmentlaw.org.uk http://www.climatechangefacts.info/ http://www.direct.gov.uk/en/Environmentandgreenerliving/Thewiderenvironment/Climatechange/index.htm	Cambridgeshire County Council http://www.cambridgeshire.gov.uk/environment/climate/climatechange+faqs.htm
climal.com http://www.climal.com/	Oxfam http://www.oxfam.org.uk/get_involved/campaign/climate_change/thailand?ito=1482&pscid=ps_ggl_GR_Climate-Change-Animation&gclid=CKTF4rr0kKYCFQ4f4QodFxtlZA
STOP CLIMATE CHAOS COALITION http://www.stopclimatechaos.org/?gclid=CNTknuD0kKYCFQZO4QodURHeZg	GreenFacts Facts on Health and the Environment http://www.greenfacts.org/en/climate-change-ar4/climate-change-ar4-foldout.pdf

www.ingramcontent.com/pod-product-compliance
Lightning Source LLC
Chambersburg PA
CBHW081803280526
45789CB00008B/2984